SCIENCE ON PATROL

In the Rainforest

Louise and
Richard Spilsbury

Gareth Stevens
PUBLISHING

Please visit our website, www.garethstevens.com.
For a free color catalog of all our high-quality books,
call toll free 1-800-542-2595 or fax 1-877-542-2596.

Cataloging-in-Publication Data

Names: Spilsbury, Louise.
Title: In the rainforest / Louise and Richard Spilsbury.
Description: New York : Gareth Stevens, 2017. | Series: Science on patrol | Includes index.
Identifiers: ISBN 9781482459807 (pbk.) | ISBN 9781482459821 (library bound) | ISBN 9781482459814 (6 pack)
Subjects: LCSH: Rain forests--Juvenile literature.
Classification: LCC QH541.5.R27 S65 2017 | DDC 577.34--dc23

First Edition

Published in 2017 by
Gareth Stevens Publishing
111 East 14th Street, Suite 349
New York, NY 10003

Copyright © 2017 Gareth Stevens Publishing

Produced for Gareth Stevens by Calcium
Editors: Sarah Eason and Jennifer Sanderson
Designers: Paul Myerscough and Simon Borrough
Picture researcher: Rachel Blount

Picture credits: Cover: Shutterstock: Aleksandar Kamasi (b), ODM (t); Inside: Conservation Drones: Sander van
Andel 34; Duke Lemur Center: Lanto Andrianandrasana 25, Kyle Smith 33; Adam Kay 23r; Johan Larson/Daintree
Rainforest Observatory: 16, 18, 19; Shutterstock: Adam Spencer 13t, Andrew M. Allport 11t, Gudkov Andrey 5,
Bikeriderlondon 28b, Rich Carey 14, Chainfoto24 1, 38–39, Andre Dib 32, Dirk Ercken 15, Steve Heap 6, Robert
Adrian Hillman 30, Ammit Jack 43, Hardeep Jaswal 35, Aleksandar Kamasi 4, Kevin H Knuth 17, Kokhanchikov 9,
Lisette van der Kroon 41, Leungchopan 7, Loca4motion 27, Lolostock 26, Margaret 12–13, Muslianshah Masrie
31, MBLifestyle 10–11, Elena Mirage 28–29t, My Good Images 21t, Naeblys 44, Dr. Morley Read 8, 20–21b, 40,
Christian Vinces 24, Voran 36–37, Wandee007 20t; Wikimedia Commons: Chad Carson 22–23, Geoff Gallice 42.

Printed in China

CPSIA compliance information: Batch #CW17GS: For further information contact Gareth Stevens, New York, New York at 1-800-542-2595.

contents

CHAPTER 1
WORKING IN THE RAINFOREST

Scientists who live and work in rainforests face many challenges. Rainforests are forests that get a huge amount of rain every year, so scientists have to cope with heat, **humidity**, rain, and sometimes deep mud. They also suffer stings and scratches from thorny plants, and bites from insects. However, their work is fascinating and vital because rainforests are Earth's oldest living **ecosystems**.

The rainforest is a challenging **habitat** to live and work in.

Where are Rainforests?

Tropical rainforests are found around the **equator**, the hottest part of the planet. This belt of Earth lies between the Tropic of Cancer and the Tropic of Capricorn. Here, temperatures and rainfall are very high all year round. Tropical rainforests are found in South and Central America, West and Central Africa, Indonesia, Southeast Asia, and tropical Australia. Almost one-third of all the remaining tropical rainforest on Earth is found in Brazil.

Gorillas live on the forest floor in the rainforest of Uganda.

Rainforest Layers

There are four layers in the tropical rainforest:

- **Emergent layer:** The tallest trees reach this highest and sunniest layer. Some are up to 200 feet (60 meters) high. Birds, butterflies, bats, and bugs live here.
- **Canopy layer:** Most trees in a rainforest have leaves and branches in this layer. The canopy forms a thick roof over the rainforest. Animals such as snakes, toucans, and tree frogs live in the canopy.
- **Understory:** Little sunshine reaches this layer, so plants here grow no taller than 12 feet (4 meters) high. They have larger leaves to receive sunlight, or they grow as vines and climb taller trees to reach the light. Animals here include frogs, many insects, and snakes.
- **Forest floor:** There are few plants on the forest floor because the leaves and branches above block out most of the light. In this damp, dark layer, leaves and other natural waste decompose quickly. Giant anteaters, jaguars, and other animals live in this layer.

5

CHALLENGES AND CHANGES

Scientists who study rainforests have buildings and labs to live and work in, but they also need to venture out on patrol. They go deep into the rainforest to collect **samples** and **data**. When they do, they face the challenges of the rainforest **climate** and finding their way in a dark jungle.

Rain in the Forest

There are no seasons in tropical rainforests. It is hot and wet all year round. All plants release water into the air through a process called **transpiration**. Rainforests are especially wet because the giant trees there release huge amounts of water. This moisture forms the clouds that hover above rainforests and make them humid and warm. When rain falls, it can be heavy and sudden. It can wash away roads and paths. It can also make rivers overflow and cause floods. Floods in the Amazon rainforest cause rivers to rise by up to 33 feet (10 meters). Floods can wash away equipment and people, and sink boats in rivers and streams.

Large volumes of water can move quickly through rainforest rivers.

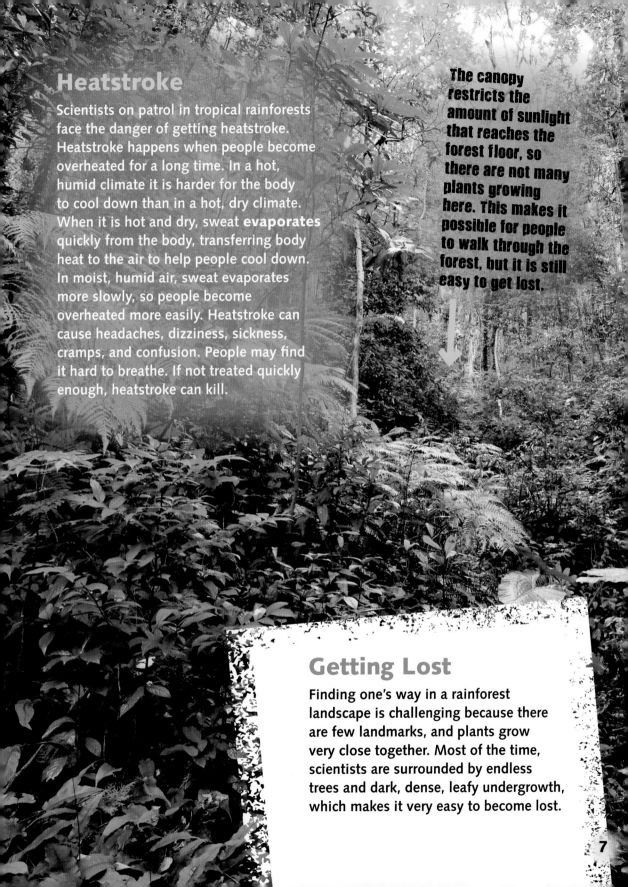

Heatstroke

Scientists on patrol in tropical rainforests face the danger of getting heatstroke. Heatstroke happens when people become overheated for a long time. In a hot, humid climate it is harder for the body to cool down than in a hot, dry climate. When it is hot and dry, sweat **evaporates** quickly from the body, transferring body heat to the air to help people cool down. In moist, humid air, sweat evaporates more slowly, so people become overheated more easily. Heatstroke can cause headaches, dizziness, sickness, cramps, and confusion. People may find it hard to breathe. If not treated quickly enough, heatstroke can kill.

The canopy restricts the amount of sunlight that reaches the forest floor, so there are not many plants growing here. This makes it possible for people to walk through the forest, but it is still easy to get lost.

Getting Lost

Finding one's way in a rainforest landscape is challenging because there are few landmarks, and plants grow very close together. Most of the time, scientists are surrounded by endless trees and dark, dense, leafy undergrowth, which makes it very easy to become lost.

Daily DANGERS

There can be more than 50,000 insect **species** in just 1 square mile (2.6 square kilometers) of rainforest and some are potentially very dangerous to humans. Mosquitoes can cause a deadly disease called malaria, and certain rainforest wasps give what may be the most painful sting in the world.

Ants, Bugs, Bees, and Wasps

As scientists walk through the rainforest, they are at risk from a variety of insects. The 1-inch (2.5 centimeter) long bullet ant has a sting so painful it feels like being shot. The bullet ant can also inject venom that can **paralyze** an ankle for hours. Vicious-looking assassin bugs deliver a bite that is both very painful and can pass on diseases that can make people very sick. Africanized honey bees attack if their nest is disturbed. A large swarm can sting a person 2,000 times. The sting of the tarantula-hawk wasp is usually used to stun tarantula spiders that the wasps eat. If one of these wasps stings a human, the pain does not last long but it is incredibly intense.

Assassin bugs are also called kissing bugs because they often bite people on the face or lips.

Mosquitoes and Malaria

Mosquitoes are insects that feed on blood. When female mosquitoes pierce skin with their long **proboscis** to drink blood, they pass disease-causing **parasites** into the human body at the same time. These parasites cause malaria. Symptoms of malaria include fever and sweating, and the disease can kill people. Mosquitoes can smell human sweat or breath up to 100 feet (30 meters) away.

A mosquito can drink up to three times its weight in blood.

SCIENCE PATROL SURVIVAL

Working in the rainforest was once very dangerous because of the risk of malaria. Then it was discovered that the bark of the cinchona tree in the Andean rainforest contained a substance called quinine. Quinine could be used to prevent and treat malaria.

Today, people visiting rainforests can take anti-malaria pills to greatly reduce their chances of getting malaria. What do you think the story of quinine tells us about how rainforest plants can help people? How might this affect what scientists study in rainforests and a country's decisions about whether rainforests should be protected? Explain your answer.

CHAPTER 2

Why Study Rainforests?

Scientists study rainforests to learn about the plants and animals here and what threatens them, and to discover new species. They also study rainforests to check the extent, causes, and impacts of **deforestation** and how rainforest deforestation affects the world's climate.

New Species

Rainforests only cover 6 percent of Earth's surface, but they contain more than half of the world's animal species and at least two-thirds of the world's plant species. Scientists estimate that they have discovered only about 6 percent of rainforest life, but on average one new rainforest species is discovered around every three days. One reason scientists hope to discover new species is that they might be useful. Rainforests are already the source of many things that people use or eat, such as rubber, avocados (pictured, right), and chocolate.

New Medicines

Rainforest plants are potentially useful for making medicines because they produce chemicals to protect themselves from disease and to ward off insects and other animals that try to eat them. Scientists study these chemicals to figure out which could be used to make medicine. A large number of medicines have already been discovered in rainforests. For example, 70 percent of the plants that have proven anticancer properties are found only in rainforests.

At least 3,000 different types of fruits are found in rainforests, so there may be many more that people can eat.

The agouti is one of very few animals that can open a Brazil nut. Agoutis are a type of rodent, so they have very sharp, strong front teeth that can gnaw into the nutshells.

Staying Put

Scientists also research which plants they can remove from the rainforest and grow elsewhere, and those that will grow only in the rainforest. For example, Brazil nut trees are useful because people eat the nuts and use oil from the nuts to make soaps, shampoos, and hair conditioners. However, Brazil nut trees will grow only in untouched areas of the Amazon rainforest. Here, rainforest bees **pollinate** the trees and new trees grow from seeds spread by small rainforest animals called agoutis.

studying plants and animals

Scientists study rainforests to learn how plants and animals survive there. Some researchers study how plants and animals interact with or rely on each other in order to understand more fully threats to jungle wildlife.

Adaptations

Scientists study **organisms** to see how they are **adapted** to live in rainforests. Rainforest soil is often shallow and low in **nutrients**, so plants have shallow roots. These shallow roots could not support a giant rainforest tree, so the trees grow wide buttress roots above the ground to prop themselves up. Orchids are epiphytes: plants that grow high on rainforest branches or trunks to reach the light. They have roots that hang in the air to collect moisture so they can grow.

Orchids are **epiphytes** that can grow on top of other plants and dangle their roots in the air.

12

Important Interactions

Some scientists research the way that hunting one animal species can cause problems for many others and can damage the rainforest ecosystem. For example, seeds need to move from their parent plant to find space to grow. When monkeys, deer, and other animals eat fruits, such as figs, they help to distribute the seeds through the forest. Some seeds are dropped after the animal eats the fruit. Others pass through the animal's guts and land somewhere new in the animal's droppings or dung. If hunters kill animals that help spread seeds, this impacts the forest. For example, hunting monkeys that eat seed-carrying fruit means there will be fewer large-seeded trees.

Monkeys and other fruit-eating animals help distribute seeds to keep rainforests healthy.

SCIENCE PATROL SURVIVAL

Bamboo is a plant that grows quickly in the gap left after a tree dies. It can spread so fast that it keeps new trees from growing. Orangutans eat bamboo stems and shoots, as well as other plants. Having many orangutans can therefore stop rainforest gaps from being taken over by bamboo. This allows rainforest trees that feed a wide variety of animals to grow there instead.

How do you think discoveries made by scientists about the roles animals play in rainforests can make a difference?

EFFECTS OF DEFORESTATION

Scientists study how cutting down rainforest trees affects the forests themselves, the climate, and the water supply. Deforestation is the clearing of forest on a massive scale. Scientists are discovering it can have some very negative effects.

Deforestation in Action

In Borneo, some rainforests are being destroyed to make space for buildings and palm oil plantations.

The Worldwide Fund for Nature estimates that 46,000 to 58,000 square miles (120,000 to 150,000 square kilometers) of rainforest are lost each year. Fires, logging for timber, and land clearing to make space for farms, ranches, buildings, airports, and golf courses can all cause deforestation. The problem is that rainforest trees are mostly hardwoods that can be slow to grow. Once rainforest trees like these are cut down, the forest does not regrow quickly or with the same tree species.

Scientific Studies

Trees release **oxygen** during the process of **photosynthesis**, by which they use sunlight to make their own food. That is why the vast rainforests of Earth are an important source of the oxygen in the **atmosphere** that people and other living things breathe. Rainforests also provide homes for people and wildlife, and many of the world's most threatened and **endangered** animals live in rainforests. Scientists study how deforestation affects the world's atmosphere, as well as the animals and people who live in the rainforest.

Climate Effects

One of the most important areas of scientific study in the rainforests is how deforestation impacts climate. During photosynthesis, trees and other plants soak up **carbon dioxide** that would otherwise stay in the atmosphere. Carbon dioxide is a greenhouse gas—one of the gases that trap warmth in the sky like glass in a greenhouse. Greenhouse gases are linked to **global warming**. Global warming is causing some places to be wetter, drier, or stormier than usual. Scientists study how deforestation may be increasing this climate change.

When forests are cut down, this reduces the habitat for rainforest animals such as this red strawberry poison dart frog.

CHAPTER 3

Lab Life

Thousands of different scientists work in the world's tropical rainforests every year, focusing on different areas of research. They work in a wide range of rainforest stations, from outdoor labs to buildings where they not only study the samples and data they collect but where they also live.

Labs on High

Some labs are erected in the rainforest trees. Scientists visit these labs during the day or night to carry out research. Canopy cranes are labs high in the sky. They give scientists a full view of more than 2 acres (8,092 square meters) of rainforest from a platform that hangs 130 feet (40 meters) above the ground from the arm of a crane. The cranes are the same as those used in cities, but they have a cage or platform hanging from their arm, with space for one or two scientists to work.

The crane jib or arm can swing round to position scientists over the particular part of the rainforest canopy they want to study.

Canopy Rafts

Some scientists work from labs that are like giant, inflatable rafts. Airships gently lower these labs onto the treetops. They rest here safely and allow scientists to move between rainforest treetops. The scientists can study the canopy without any risk of damaging branches and the plants and animals that live and grow there. Some canopy rafts are large enough to hold as many as eight or ten scientists.

Scientists have used canopy walkways like this, strung between high treetops, to study the rainforest. Today, such walkways are more often used by tourists.

Tall Towers

Scientists also study rainforest canopies from the top of large wooden towers. These towers can be about 5 feet square (0.5 meter square) at the base and about 150 feet (46 meters) tall. They are anchored to the ground with strong wires to make them stable. Scientists climb ladders to reach the research platforms that are placed at different levels on the tower.

Research Stations

Research or base stations are groups of permanent buildings where scientists live. They contain labs where scientists work, and they are also the bases to where scientists return after spending days on canopy cranes, towers, or rafts, or carrying out other forms of research in the rainforest.

Building Bases

Research base stations are sometimes built on the edge of a rainforest so they are easy to reach. They can also be deep inside the forest, so scientists are closer to untouched areas of trees that they can study. They are usually built from local timber and are often surrounded by fences to keep out wild animals. These fences are made from wood or smooth wire that will not injure wildlife. Importantly, the stations must have a watertight roof to keep out heavy rainfall and prevent both the scientists and their expensive equipment from being soaked.

These scientists are completing research in an outdoor work area of the Daintree Rainforest Observatory (DRO) in Australia.

Inside a Research Station

Research stations vary in size. Some have one building that contains a lab, a small dormitory, and a bathroom and kitchen for scientists. Others may look like small villages made up of several buildings. These may have several labs with equipment scientists can use to study insects, plants, and other organisms they find outdoors, and separate cabins or buildings for scientists to live, sleep, cook, eat, and relax in. They may also have offices, a library and reading rooms with scientific books, journals, and computers, and visitor centers.

A scientist at the DRO checks and studies insects collected in the rainforest.

SCIENCE PATROL SURVIVAL

To study the rainforest canopy, scientists in the past would chop down the trees or use chemical sprays to stun or even kill animals so they fell to the forest floor where they could be studied more easily.

Why do you think it is important that scientists today use cranes, rafts, and platforms to allow them to view the canopy? Explain why this matters and how you think it helps the scientists get a more accurate picture of life in a rainforest.

Research Stations at Work

Research stations need electricity to power equipment and computers. They need food supplies and fuel for cooking. They also need systems for scientists to communicate with the outside world, both to share results of their research and in case there is an emergency.

Supplying the Station

Some of the supplies needed in a research station arrive by boat along rainforest rivers. Other supplies are dropped from planes or are driven to a nearby road by jeep, and have to be carried to the camp. Many stations have **solar panels** to supply the electricity they need to power lights and other machines. Solar panels capture the energy in the sunshine, and convert it into electricity. Usually, research stations use local materials to build labs and other rooms instead of bringing in materials from elsewhere. This is because transporting materials causes **pollution** from vehicle exhausts. Bringing in materials would also require more roads to be built, which would mean cutting down more trees.

These workers are building a new road through the Amazon rainforest.

Some satellite phones have Global Positioning System (GPS) so they can help scientists find their way around and communicate from remote locations.

Reducing Impacts

Scientists take measures to ensure that their research stations and their activities do not impact the rainforest environment negatively. Pollution and waste can damage both wildlife and the habitats they live in, so any waste the stations produce is removed or disposed of carefully. For example, they collect waste such as plastic packaging or bottles, which might trap and harm rainforest animals, and transport it out of the jungle.

Keeping in Touch

Labs in the rainforest are very far away from cell-phone towers, so scientists have difficulty getting signals. Instead, they use **satellite** phones. Satellite phones can be used anywhere in the world to transmit and receive signals to and from satellites high in the atmosphere above Earth. The phones are small and light, making it easy for scientists to carry them in their packs when they go out to work in the rainforest.

Take a Tour

The Smithsonian Tropical Research Institute (STRI) has a permanent research station located on the island of Barro Colorado in Lake Gatun, which is in the middle of the Panama Canal. Hundreds of scientists come to Barro Colorado station each year to use its labs to study the rainforest.

Barro Colorado

Barro Colorado is almost six times bigger than Manhattan's Central Park and is part of an important nature reserve. The island is home to an undisturbed tropical rainforest with thousands of species of animals and plants. Park guards watch over the island to ensure that no logging or poaching takes place. The first field station on the island was built in 1928. Over the years, thousands of scientists have worked here. Much of what is known about tropical rainforests comes from this island.

Buildings on Barro Colorado

Barro Colorado has modern laboratory buildings that are air conditioned to make them comfortable for scientists working in the heat. There are buildings for growing plants and an insectary for keeping and rearing insects to study. There is a room where scientists can control light levels to study nocturnal animals and insects, which are active at night and rest during the daytime.

High-Tech Facilities

There are seven radio towers on the island that track tagged animals and send data to one of the computer rooms on the site that has Internet access. There is a lecture and conference room, where scientists can give and hear talks, and discuss their research. Barro Colorado also has living areas where scientists stay, a kitchen, and a dining hall. For visitors who arrive at Barro Colorado's dock by boat, there is a cafeteria and a visitor center with displays about Barro Colorado.

Scientists need room to store and study the rainforest samples that they collect.

The scientists who have visited the Barro Colorado research station over the past 80 years have made the rainforest here among the most studied in the world.

23

CHAPTER 4

OUT and About

Scientists travel by different means when they go out on patrol. When they leave their research base station, it can take several challenging hours to reach the site where they want to set up equipment and study.

Traveling by Boat

Rainforests get a huge amount of rainfall each year, so it is hardly surprising that they have some of the largest rivers in the world. The Amazon River, for example, accounts for 16 percent of the total amount of water discharged by rivers into the world's oceans. Many scientists travel to and from their base stations by boat. They may arrive at a base station by ferry and use canoes, kayaks, or motorboats to carry equipment and supplies to remote research sites.

Scientists use the numerous waterways, streams, and rivers in a rainforest to get deep into the jungle.

Rugged Roads

There are some roads into and through rainforests, but they are few and far between. Scientists on patrol are more likely to be driving on rough, mud tracks, so the most commonly used vehicle is a jeep or 4x4. These have large wheels that hold the body of the vehicle well above the wet ground. Many rainforest tracks have deep, wide holes that are usually filled with rainwater. These can damage vehicles that drive into them. Scientists have to ensure they carry tools to mend their vehicles if they get damaged on the journey.

Traveling on foot is the most environmentally friendly way to explore the rainforest. It causes the least damage and disruption, and no pollution.

Long-Distance Walking

Most of the time, a boat or vehicle can get scientists only so far, so they often travel on foot. To go deep into a rainforest with trees that grow closely together and dense undergrowth, the only option is to walk. Thick vines and leafy branches often block trails, so scientists on patrol carry knives to cut a path through the vegetation.

25

SURVIVAL GEAR

When scientists leave the comfort of a base station and set out on patrol, they need to wear clothing, boots, and other gear that will keep them safe from the intense sun, heat, and dampness in the rainforest, and from the biting bugs that are always ready to attack.

Light and Long

Most scientists wear light, long-sleeved tops and long trousers made of fabrics that dry quickly in the humid rainforest habitat. Jeans are inappropriate because, when they get wet in the rainforest, they can take days to dry out. Many people opt for khaki or brown clothes. These colors are good for **camouflage** and in a muddy, puddle-filled rainforest, most clothes end up these colors after a short time! Long sleeves and trousers shade the skin from the sun. People put sunblock on any skin that is not covered to prevent painful sunburn.

A wide-brimmed hat keeps the sun off the face, preventing sunburn and making it easier to see.

Beating the Bugs

Long-sleeved tops and long trousers also help protect skin from being bitten by the bugs that are everywhere in the rainforest. Scientists on patrol also use insect repellent sprays or liquids. They apply these to their skin, especially around the ankles, to keep insects away. Another option is to rub mud onto the skin. The mud dries to form a crust that insects cannot bite through.

Long-sleeved tops and long trousers also help protect people from the scratches and rashes thorny or poisonous plants cause.

Avoiding Foot Rot

Wet feet are a constant problem in the rainforest. If feet do not have a chance to dry out, people can get foot rot. The feet become covered in red sores and feel as if they are on fire. It becomes too painful to walk. To avoid this, researchers wear waterproof boots, put on a dry pair of socks each morning, and try to let their feet dry out fully each night.

Being Prepared

A large part of scientists' attention in a rainforest is focused on coping with the environment: finding their way around and keeping safe and healthy. To do this, they must ensure they have the correct supplies, medicines, and navigation equipment.

Packing Supplies

As scientists are likely to be walking for at least part of the day, they need to fit supplies in a backpack. They must try to keep the pack light, because carrying a heavy pack will make them tired more quickly and make them hotter. As well as a basic first-aid kit and insect repellent, they take a waterproof poncho or coat to keep them dry when there is heavy rainfall. Dried or canned foods stay fresh, and high-energy foodstuffs, such as granola bars, are small and light to carry. No pack is complete without some navigation equipment such as a **compass** or GPS unit.

A scientist's backpack usually contains anything from a simple torch to a high-tech GPS unit.

Getting Water

There is a lot of freshwater in rainforests. The problem is that the water in streams, pools, and rivers is often **contaminated**. It can be dirty and contain parasites that make people sick. Water is heavy to carry and takes up a lot of space, so scientists on patrol often take water purifying tablets instead. These kill any harmful organisms in the water. Scientists can also use a water treatment device, such as a **filter**, which will kill most bugs.

To prevent heatstroke in a rainforest, people should drink a lot of water, even when they do not feel thirsty.

SCIENCE PATROL SURVIVAL

Scientists working in the rainforest have to keep a constant lookout for wildlife. In rainforest rivers there could be piranhas. These dangerous fish attack in groups and have razor-sharp, triangular teeth that can strip flesh down to the bone in minutes. Jaguars are large wild cats that may attack humans if they feel cornered and have no escape route, or if they are injured.

How do you think dealing with these daily challenges might affect scientists as they work? Give reasons for your answers.

CAMPING OUT

Scientists on patrol may travel so far from their base station to collect samples and data that they have to stay in the rainforest overnight or longer. That means they have to set up a camp to work and to sleep, eat, and relax in.

Sleeping in a hammock keeps people off the rainforest floor and away from insects and snakes.

Shelter

Scientists often take some sort of tarpaulin with them to provide shade during the day when they are working, eating, or resting. It does get very hot in the jungle and it is best to be out of the sun during the hottest part of the day. A shelter is even more important at night. Night comes early in the rainforest, when it becomes completely dark. Rains can fall suddenly. Tents should be small, lightweight, and completely waterproof. Scientists also usually carry a waterproof sleeping bag, just in case any water gets into the tent.

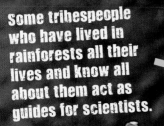

Some tribespeople who have lived in rainforests all their lives and know all about them act as guides for scientists.

Bed Bugs

A shelter also protects scientists from insects and other rainforest animals. Sleeping on an inflatable mattress or a hammock keeps people off the forest floor where insects scuttle about. If sleeping outside a tent, scientists use a mosquito net. A mosquito net has tiny holes that allow people to breathe and see out of, but keep insects from getting in. At night, people hang up clothes and boots to keep bugs from crawling into them. They must check clothes and footwear carefully for insects before putting them on again in the morning.

Rainforest Guides

On longer rainforest treks, scientists often travel with a local guide from an **indigenous** rainforest tribe. Guides help scientists find their way around, avoid dangers, and choose safe places to camp. It is best to make camp away from rivers to avoid floods. Insects, such as mosquitoes, also gather near water and wild animals come to rivers to drink. Guides can spot things like rotten trees from which branches could suddenly fall, damaging a camp or injuring people sleeping inside. Guides usually know the land well and know where there are rock crevices and hollow logs or burrows where snakes might be lurking.

31

CHAPTER 5

CUTTING-EDGE TECHNOLOGY

Scientists studying in the rainforest rely on a variety of technology to help them locate and study not only the animals hidden among the trees, but also the rainforest habitat and how it is changing.

Tracking Devices

Studying wildlife often requires scientists to follow individual animals. One way scientists do this is capturing an animal and attaching a harmless radio-tracking device to it, sometimes on a collar or leg band. The device produces a signal that is detected by a series of towers around the rainforest. Each tower automatically relays how strong, or near, the signal is to a computer. Computers combine all the data from the towers to pinpoint the animal's position. Researchers can then see patterns in the animal's position, such as routes it takes, where it stops, or places it avoids. Tracking can also be done by following the location of devices using GPS. GPS is a system that figures out where something is on Earth by comparing its position to the fixed positions of satellites in space.

A jaguar has to be sedated before it can be fitted with a collar equipped with a GPS device, which will track it as it moves about in its habitat.

This scientist is using a radio tracker to trace a greater dwarf lemur in the Madagascan rainforest.

Camera Traps

Tracking can be done only on a limited number of animals that have tracking devices fitted. As an alternative, scientists sit in a hide and watch animals to understand where they live and what they do. Hours in hot, bug-infested conditions can be demanding for researchers, so they also set up camouflaged cameras that are automatically triggered when approaching animals break an **infrared** light switch. Images or video sequences captured day or night by these camera traps can be saved on data cards and retrieved later by scientists. The data can be transmitted automatically by cell phone to a computer back in the lab.

Rainforest Robots

Scientists are increasingly turning to flying robots to help them study rainforests. Unmanned aerial vehicles (UAVs) have no pilot on board and are either mini-helicopters with many spinning rotors or small airplanes. UAVs are also known as drones. Drones have battery-powered motors. People on the ground use handsets that resemble video game controllers to steer them. They can see where their drones are going via a digital camera that transmits live video to a computer screen.

Scientists use drones to move through and above trees to spot and count different types of animals and plants, and witness their lives and interactions.

Drones and Elephants

While working with drones, scientists made an interesting discovery. Elephants hate the buzzing sound that the UAVs make. Whenever they hear a drone in the sky, they run in the opposite direction. Although scientists are not certain why this happens, they believe it is because elephants think the sound comes from an approaching swarm of bees. With this new knowledge, some **conservationists** are starting to use drones to scare away elephants from areas where there are traps and poachers. They would prefer not to worry wild animals, but at least this keeps the elephants safe.

Counting Orangutans

The island of Sumatra in Indonesia is one of the last places where wild orangutans live. However, deforestation threatens them. Today, there are fewer than 7,000 of these fascinating apes left in an area of 180,000 square miles (466,198 square kilometers). On foot, trudging through swamps and up mountains in the rainforest, days can go by without scientists spotting a single ape. So scientists are now using drones to fly just above the canopy. High-resolution images from the drones are helping scientists spot the apes and their nests tucked among the treetops.

Remote Sensing

Remote sensing is getting information about an area from a great distance away. Scientists learn much about the state of rainforests through remote sensing from satellites in space.

How Remote Sensing Works

Machines on satellites, including **radar** and **lasers**, send beams of energy toward Earth. They have sensitive apparatus that records how much of that energy is reflected back to space and how long it takes. The data are used to create maps of anything from where there are rainforests on our planet to what plants they are composed of and how healthy the plants are. For example, plants that contain more moisture or are greener reflect energy better than drier or more yellow plants.

Monitoring Rainforest Change

Images taken by cameras on satellites can spot areas of deforestation and also places where the rainforest is growing back after having been cleared. However, cloud cover can spoil satellite views of rainforest. Healthy rainforest has vegetation at different levels and of different types of plant. Checking what the rainforest is actually like is possible on foot, but this process is far too time-consuming. Instead, computer software uses digital images of the forest from different angles and heights to create 3D pictures of rainforests. These images help scientists monitor rainforest change.

The brown patches in this satellite image show where trees have been cut down in an area of rainforest.

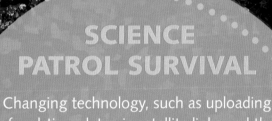

SCIENCE
PATROL SURVIVAL

Changing technology, such as uploading of real-time data via satellite links and the Internet, is helping rainforest scientists share their specific findings more quickly with other scientists, conservation organizations, governments, and the general public.

Give an example of this and explain how you think communication improvements are helping rainforests now and how they will help in the future.

Climate Technology

Rainforest weather and climate patterns are studied using a variety of technology. This ranges from simple rain gauges to complex carbon **sensors**.

Rainforest Weather Stations

To get a full idea of the weather across a whole rainforest, scientists have to carry weather measuring technology into the deepest, most remote parts of jungles. Rain gauges are simple devices that often consist of nothing more than a funnel and a bottle, usually in a metal casing. The funnel channels rainwater into the bottle, and scientists return each morning to measure how much rainfall has fallen in the previous 24 hours. Scientists also need to find out how heat, air, and water vapor circulate inside the forest canopy, so they set up special sensors in the canopy that measure humidity, temperature, and **solar radiation**.

The water vapor that trees release hangs above the rainforest in clouds.

Trees and Carbon Dioxide

Scientists study how rainforest trees use carbon dioxide using sensitive technology. They build towers up to 150 feet (50 meters) tall in forests. These are studded with delicate sensors that measure the proportion of carbon dioxide and water vapor in the air, as well as wind speed. The scientists see if a rise in carbon dioxide makes rainforest trees grow faster and whether warmer temperatures are causing trees to release more moisture. Together with wind speeds, this affects cloud formation and weather patterns. Future carbon dioxide levels could be much higher than today. Scientists test future levels by pumping carbon dioxide over an area of trees surrounded by the towers to see how this affects trees.

SCIENCE PATROL SURVIVAL

It is so hot and humid in the rainforest that maintaining scientific equipment can be challenging. Water vapor can get into machines and keep them from working properly. Insects can get inside and damage electronic devices.

How do you think this affects scientists working in the rainforest?

CHAPTER 6

AMAZING DISCOVERIES

One of the most amazing and significant discoveries scientists have made about rainforests is the extent to which rainforests affect the world's climate. They have discovered that rainforests are a vital force shaping the world's weather and climate patterns by helping control gases, temperature, and water levels in the atmosphere.

Carbon Sinks

Scientists have discovered that rainforests play an important role in controlling climate change because they act as **carbon sinks**. In fact, rainforests are one of the largest stores of carbon dioxide on Earth. The problem is that the amount of carbon that rainforests are absorbing from the atmosphere and storing is falling. Scientists have learned that, in the past, increased amounts of carbon dioxide in the atmosphere encouraged photosynthesis. Rainforest trees took in more carbon dioxide and grew even bigger and faster, creating more useful carbon sinks. However, the trees reach maturity faster and die sooner, which keeps them from taking in more carbon dioxide.

The global climate depends on the Amazon rainforest.

The Feedback Loop

Scientists have also discovered another problem. Deforestation, forest fires, and **droughts**, which are probably caused by global warming, are also destroying or damaging rainforest trees. When the trees are cut down or die, carbon once stored inside the trees is released as they rot or are burned. This extra carbon dioxide released into the atmosphere contributes to global warming. This creates a feedback loop—more trees dying means more global warming, which means more trees dying. This could have catastrophic effects on the climate.

Deforestation around the world is already responsible for up to one-fifth of global greenhouse gas emissions.

Rainforests and Rain

Scientists have also made an important discovery about the way in which deforestation impacts rainfall patterns. Rainforests release vast amounts of water vapor and generate clouds and rain. When rainforests are lost, less water is released into the atmosphere and fewer clouds form. In rainforests, this means streams and soils dry out and plants die. The loss of rainforests and the rain they create could lead to droughts and crop failures elsewhere in the world.

SPECIES CONSERVATION

In a 2012 expedition to a remote rainforest in Surinam, South America, scientists discovered 60 new species, including 6 new frogs and 28 new bats. This is an example of the amazing discoveries adding to our knowledge of global rainforest **biodiversity**.

Plant Discoveries

Some discoveries are enormous. In 2015, scientists discovered a new, giant tree in the African rainforest weighing about 105 tons (95 tonnes)! Some new species are important because of what they could do for people. For example, a new type of mushroom found in Ecuador can decompose (break down) a type of plastic called polyurethane. This tough material is used to make things such as carpets, shoes, and backyard hoses. In the future, this mushroom might be used to help decompose the vast piles of waste that humans have created across the planet.

Species Loss

Scientists hope to discover more new species, like this bug, before too much rainforest is lost.

Many biologists expect that rainforests will lose 5 to 10 percent of their species each decade, even newly discovered ones. Poaching is one of the causes of species loss in areas of forest. For example, a major reason that great apes such as chimps are endangered is that poachers kill them for meat. Scientists call these animals keystone

species because they are essential to the rest of the forest. They disperse seeds of many trees, upon which other animals feed. Scientists assess the impact of poaching but also work to prevent it. Some special camera traps placed in rainforests not only secretly take pictures of poachers but also have special sensors that can detect vibrations in the ground caused by people walking nearby.

Conservation

Scientists advise communities and governments on how best to conserve rainforests. They help decide, for example, how much space different species need in protected reserves. They also help educate local people on how to look after the forests sustainably. This means replanting trees and making sure that forest products, such as wood, Brazil nuts, or honey, are harvested in a way that leaves the forest healthy and productive.

Scientists are studying how tourists in rainforests impact the habitat and its plants and wildlife.

PATROLLING the future

In the future, the work science patrols carry out in rainforests is going to become even more important. Their discoveries could have a profound impact on the future of the planet.

Using Discoveries

Scientists are discovering that the loss of rainforests is making global warming worse and is leading to increased deforestation. By sharing this information with other scientists, they can test that their discoveries are valid. A large number of scientists have gathered data and information that suggest that halting and reversing deforestation will help reduce the impacts of global warming. This makes governments more likely to take action to reduce deforestation. They might, for example, make laws that force companies to produce goods, such as beef, soy, palm oil, and paper, in ways that have a minimal impact on rainforests.

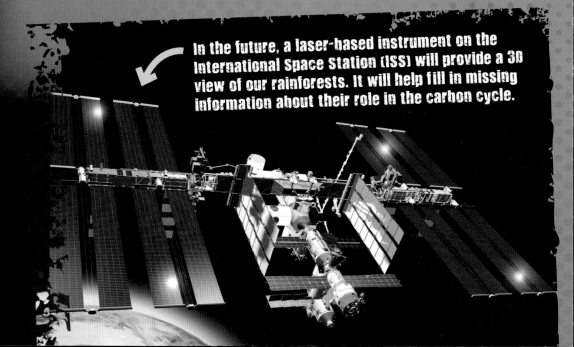

In the future, a laser-based instrument on the International Space Station (ISS) will provide a 3D view of our rainforests. It will help fill in missing information about their role in the carbon cycle.

Future Technologies

Scientists are always looking to improve the technologies with which they gather data. For example, from 2018 Lidar technology aboard the ISS will be used to measure exactly how many tons of carbon-storing wood there are per acre in rainforests. Lidar technology beams pulses of laser light to a target and analyzes how it bounces back. This enables scientists to figure out a highly detailed image of the distribution of wood in forests and how it changes. Using equipment that can improve the accuracy of results will help scientists' understanding of problems such as deforestation and global warming, and enable them to solve them.

SCIENCE PATROL SURVIVAL

Working in rainforests is challenging, difficult, and sometimes even dangerous. Scientists need somewhere to work productively and live and relax comfortably. Imagine you are going to design your own rainforest research station. What will you include there?

- *Will your station consist of several buildings or only one?*
- *How many labs will you include and what will they be used to study?*
- *How will the station be powered?*
- *What vehicles will scientists be able to use for moving around?*
- *What recreation facilities will you include?*

Glossary

adapted having features that make something suitable to a life in a particular habitat

atmosphere a blanket of gases around a planet

biodiversity the variety of plant and animal life in a particular habitat or ecosystem

camouflage features of an animal's skin or fur that helps it hide in its habitat

carbon dioxide a gas in the atmosphere that is linked to global warming

carbon sinks things that absorb more carbon than they release

climate the usual pattern of weather that happens in a place

compass a device with a magnetized pointer that shows the direction of north

conservationists people who work to protect the environment, habitats, plants, and wildlife of the world

contaminated dirty with germs or poisonous

data facts and statistics

deforestation the cutting down and removal of all or most of the trees in a forest

droughts when an area gets so little water or rain that plants die

ecosystems communities of plants and animals and the habitats they live in

endangered in danger of dying out and becoming extinct

epiphytes plants that grow on other plants for support, usually to get up high to reach sunlight

equator an imaginary line around the middle of the planet

evaporates turns from liquid into a gas

filter to pass something such as water through a mesh to remove dirt

Global Positioning System (GPS) a system that uses signals from satellites in space to locate positions on Earth

global warming changes in the world's weather patterns caused by human activity

habitat a place in nature where animals live

humidity having a lot of moisture in the air

indigenous describes living things that have belonged to a place for the longest time

infrared a type of light that is invisible

lasers narrow, highly concentrated light beams

nutrients substances that living things need to grow and be healthy

organisms living things

oxygen a gas in the atmosphere that living things need to breathe

paralyze to make something unable to move

parasites animals or plants that live in or on another animal or plant and get food from it

photosynthesis the process by which plants make food from carbon dioxide and water using energy from sunlight

pollinate when pollen from one plant gets to another plant of the same kind so that seeds will be produced

pollution when air, soil, or water are spoiled or made dirty or harmful by something else

proboscis a long, sucking mouthpart

radar a way of finding the position of an object by bouncing a radio wave off it and analyzing the reflected wave

samples representative parts or single items from a larger whole or group

satellite an electronic device high in space that moves around Earth

sensors devices that detect and measure something such as amounts of a particular gas in the air

solar panels panels designed to absorb the sun's rays and use them to make electricity

solar radiation all of the light and energy that comes from the sun

species a type of plant or animal

transpiration the process by which plants absorb water through roots, then give off water vapor through pores in their leaves

water vapor when water is a gas in the air. Water comes in three states: ice (solid), water (liquid), and water vapor (gas).

For More Information

Books

DK Eyewitness Books. *The Amazon*. New York: Dorling Kindersley, 2015.

Ganeri, Anita. *Bloomin' Rainforests* (Horrible Geography).
New York, NY: Scholastic Press, 2015.

Rainforests (Visual Explorers). Hauppauge, NY:
Barron's Educational Series, 2015.

Remarkable Rainforests: Everything you want to know about the world's rainforest regions in one amazing book (It's all about...). New York, NY:
Kingfisher, 2016.

Royston, Angela. *Rainforest Food Chains* (Young Explorer: Food Chains and Webs). North Mankato, MN: Raintree, 2015.

Websites

There is a wealth of rainforest information at:
http://kids.mongabay.com

Explore the rainforests of the world with National Geographic at:
environment.nationalgeographic.com/environment/habitats/ rainforest-profile

Watch a fascinating video about Barro Colorado Island at:
www.youtube.com/watch?v=tRGG-XmNMhk

Publisher's note to educators and parents: Our editors have carefully reviewed these websites to ensure that they are suitable for students. Many websites change frequently, however, and we cannot guarantee that a site's future contents will continue to meet our high standards of quality and educational value. Be advised that students should be closely supervised whenever they access the Internet.

index